Let's Add Up!

$$5 + 5 = 10$$

Victoria Allenby

Illustrated by Maggie Zeng

pajamapress

5 drums + 5 tambourines = 10 instruments…

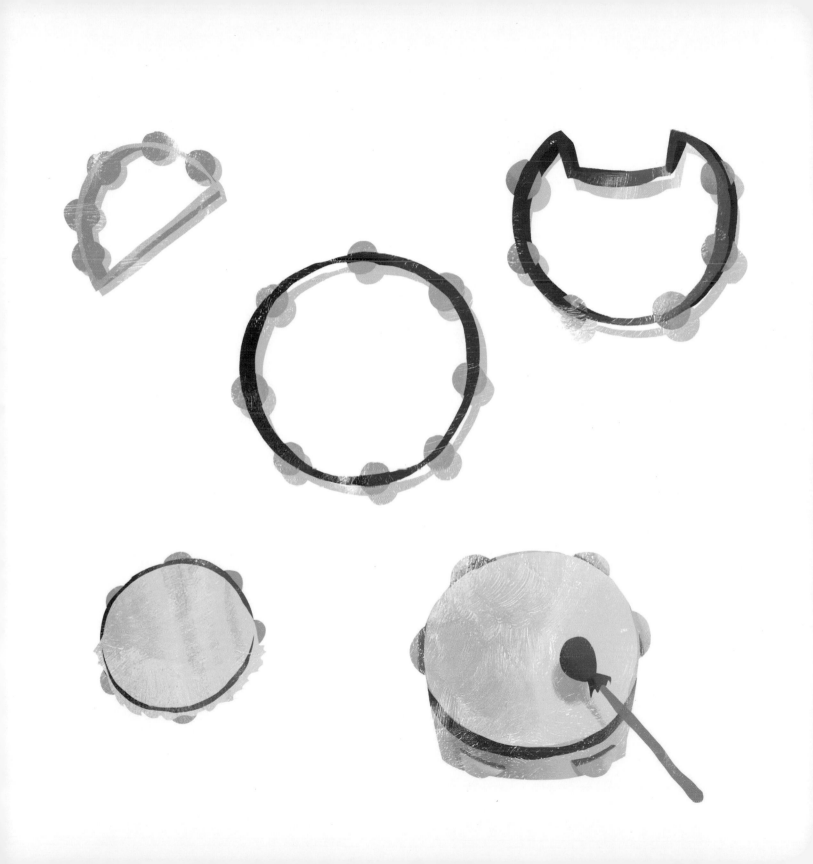

...or a **band**!

6 pots **+ 4** pans **= 10** dishes…

...or a **feast!**

7 capes **+ 3** robes **= 10** costumes…

...or a **play!**

8 cars + 2 trucks = 10 vehicles...

...or a **race**!

9 kids **+ 1** more **= 10** friends...

...or a **party!**

Classification and composing the number 10 are both foundational early math skills. Make learning fun by trying these activities with your child.

1. Classify other items with your child. For example, apples and bananas are both **fruit**. Socks and shirts are both **clothing**.

2. You can show all the ways to add up to 10 using **10** large beads strung loosely on a string. For example, as you read "6 pots + 4 pans," help your child move the beads so that **6** are on the left and **4** are on the right.

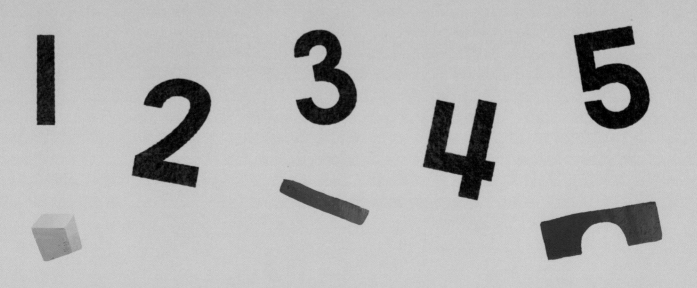

3. Go on a **#10** hunt with your child. You can find and count **10** fingers and **10** toes, then look for other groups of **10** items around your home.

4. Challenge your child's creativity with other groups of objects. "What can we do with **2** cylinders and **8** cubes?"

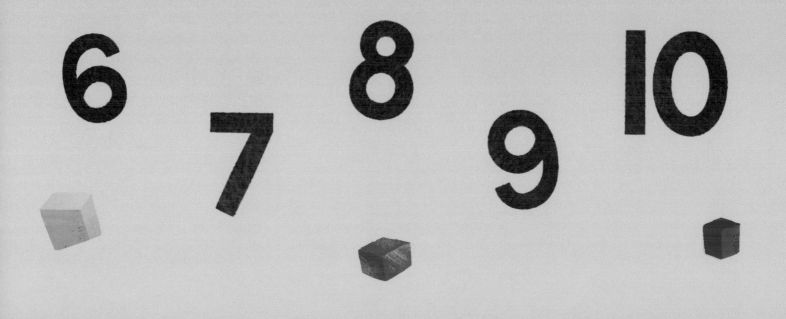

First published in Canada and the United States in 2022

Text copyright © 2022 Victoria Allenby
Illustration copyright © 2022 Maggie Zeng
This edition copyright © 2022 Pajama Press Inc.
This is a first edition.

10 9 8 7 6 5 4 3 2 1

www.pajamapress.ca   info@pajamapress.ca

 Canada Council Conseil des arts
for the Arts du Canada

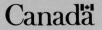 ONTARIO ARTS COUNCIL
CONSEIL DES ARTS DE L'ONTARIO
an Ontario government agency
un organisme du gouvernement de l'Ontario

Canadä

The publisher gratefully acknowledges the support of the Canada Council for the Arts and the Ontario Arts Council for its publishing program. We acknowledge the financial support of the Government of Canada through the Canada Book Fund (CBF) for our publishing activities.

Library and Archives Canada Cataloguing in Publication
Title: Let's add up! / Victoria Allenby ; illustrated by Maggie Zeng.
Other titles: Let us add up!
Names: Allenby, Victoria, 1989- author. | Zeng, Maggie, illustrator.
Description: First edition.
Identifiers: Canadiana 20220186294 | ISBN 9781772782486 (hardcover)
Subjects: LCSH: Addition—Juvenile literature. | LCSH: Arithmetic—Juvenile literature.
Classification: LCC QA115 .A45 2022 | DDC j513.2/11—dc23

Publisher Cataloging-in-Publication Data (U.S.)
Names: Allenby, Victoria, 1989-, author. | Zeng, Maggie, illustrator.
Title: Let's Add Up! / Victoria Allenby ; illustrated by Maggie Zeng.
Description: Toronto, Ontario Canada : Pajama Press, 2022.
Identifiers: ISBN 978-1-77278-248-6 (hardcover)
Subjects: LCSH: Arithmetic – Juvenile literature. | Counting – Juvenile literature. | BISAC: JUVENILE NONFICTION / Concepts / Counting & Numbers. | JUVENILE NONFICTION / Mathematics / Arithmetic. | JUVENILE NONFICTION / Toys, Dolls & Puppets.
Classification: LCC QA107.2A454 | DDC 513 – dc23

Original art created digitally
Cover and book design— Lorena González Guillén

Printed in China by WKT Company

Pajama Press Inc.
11 Davies Avenue, Suite 103, Toronto, Ontario Canada, M4M 2A9

Distributed in Canada by UTP Distribution
5201 Dufferin Street Toronto, Ontario Canada, M3H 5T8

Distributed in the U.S. by Ingram Publisher Services
1 Ingram Blvd. La Vergne, TN 37086, USA

For my sister
–V.A.

To my mom and dad,
who taught me how
to count
–M.Z.